CYCLING ON
BY RAY HALLETT

Illustrated by John Holder

Published for The National Trust
by
Dinosaur Publications Ltd
Over Cambridge England

© 1978 Ray Hallett & John Holder   ISBN/85122/156/4

The ancestors of the modern bicycle were first made in France at the end of the eighteenth century. They were called hobby horses and were propelled by pushing on the ground with the feet. They soon appeared in England, where they were also known as dandy horses, and for a time fashionable young men could be seen riding them in Hyde Park or along the Mall in London. It was possible to go quite quickly on level ground and although their boots were soon worn out, some riders managed to cover considerable distances. Someone suggested issuing hobby horses to postmen but the idea came to nothing, probably because to most people the hobby horse was nothing more than a joke.

The first real bicycle was invented in 1839 by Kirkpatric Macmillan, who was a blacksmith in Dumfries. It was driven by treadles connected to the rear wheel and it must have been a very good machine, because Macmillan often rode long distances. He was once unlucky enough to knock over a child in Glasgow at the end of a forty-mile ride. He was fined five shillings by a magistrate who certainly disapproved of such a strange and dangerous contraption.

Although a number of similar machines were built, for a time the idea of riding on two wheels seems to have been almost forgotten. Instead, a variety of primitive tricycles and enormous four-wheelers, called *Quadricycles*, were built. These were never really successful because they were so heavy and clumsy.

A new type of bicycle, called the Velocipede, appeared in the early 1860s although some early examples were shown at The Great Exhibition in 1851. Like the hobby horse, Velocipedes were made of wood and iron and they were very heavy. On the rough roads of the 1860s, riding a Velocipede was hard, uncomfortable work and they became known as 'boneshakers' which described them perfectly. Unlike Macmillan's bicycle, the boneshaker was driven by cranks and pedals connected to the front wheel. A rear-wheel brake was connected by a cord to the handlebar which had to be rotated to operate the brake.

The 'improved boneshaker' was lighter and had solid rubber tyres instead of iron ones. However, it still needed a great deal of effort to pedal very far and most riders were content to make short trips. A few 'veloci-pedists' were more adventurous and 1869 three men managed to ride from London to Brighton. 'The Times' reported on their 'astounding feat':

"On Wednesday, Mr John Mayall, son of the well-known photographer, accomplished the journey from London to Brighton on one of the new two-wheeled velocipedes; he was accompanied by two friends, Mr Charles Spencer and Mr Turner, also on two-wheeled velocipedes. They had a preliminary run round Trafalgar Square and started off at a rate of eight miles an hour on roads which proved to be generally good against a strong head wind all the way. They kept together pretty close as far as Crawley (30 miles) after which Mr Mayall took a decided lead and arrived in Brighton, and his two friends shortly after, all in good condition for dinner and the second part of a concert at the Grand Hall."

The 53-mile journey took fourteen hours. Unfortunately for the velocipedists, two men walked the same distance a few days later in eleven hours. Two months later, however, another rider who was a skating champion, and probably had a favourable wind, completed the journey in $7\frac{1}{2}$ hours at an average speed of 7 m.p.h.

Going round corners on a boneshaker was awkward and could be dangerous because the driving wheel tended to rub against the rider's legs when turned either way. Mudguards, which would have prevented this from happening, had not yet been thought of. The 'Phantom' of 1869 was an attempt to overcome the problem. Instead of turning the front wheel, the frame was steered from the middle. Both wheels followed the same arc when cornering and the front wheel stayed in line with the rider. Wooden spokes were replaced by steel ones which made the wheels stronger and much lighter. The 'Phantom' was an improvement on the boneshaker but it was a difficult machine to get used to because of its peculiar steering.

In 1871, James Starley invented a completely new kind of bicycle called the 'Ariel'. It had a much larger driving wheel than the Phantom and a very small rear wheel. Both wheels had metal rims and spokes and the frame was a simple spine connecting the rear wheel to the steering head. The Ariel was the first High bicycle, and later machines of this type were called 'Ordinaries' to distinguish them from modern safety bicycles. Most people today call them 'Penny-farthings'.

The Ariel was the first really efficient bicycle and marks the point in the history of cycling when the bicycle became a practical form of transport. A rider could outpace a man on a horse and could ride a hundred miles or more in a day. The only other way such a distance could be covered so quickly was by train. The boneshaker was soon forgotten and the High bicycle became 'King of the Road'.

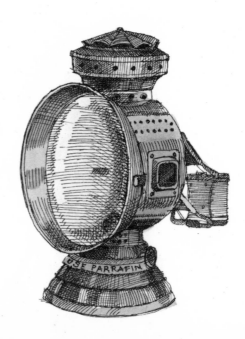

The driving wheels of high bicycles varied in size to suit different riders. A man 5′ 8″ tall normally rode a 54″ wheel, and 60″ wheels were made for really tall men. Attempting to back-pedal was the only way to slow down and roadster models were also fitted with a spoon brake which pressed down on the front tyre. A powerful ground brake was sometimes fitted and was very useful in an emergency. It dragged under the rear wheel and was similar to devices used on horse-drawn vehicles.

It required skill and nerve to ride a high bicycle. Mounting the saddle was an art in itself, but beginners found it even more difficult to get off safely. Descending a hill could be dangerous because the rider was seated high up over the front wheel and could be thrown over the handlebars if the brake was applied too suddenly or if the front wheel ran into a rut.

The skill needed to ride a high bicycle was certainly one of its attractions and it became something of a cult among athletic young men. Captain Crawley's "Art of Bicycle Riding", written in 1876, described various tricks for advanced riders – riding side saddle, standing on the saddle and how to jump on and off while in motion.

During the twenty years that these machines were in fashion, engineering techniques improved rapidly. Hollow steel tubes were used for frames and forks instead of the solid iron of a few years earlier. Hollow wheel rims and ball bearings made wheels lighter and much smoother running. Some racers built for racing on the 'path' or track weighed as little as 20lb which is much lighter than most modern machines.

There were many different makes and models of cycle to choose from. Some of the cheapest were hardly worth riding while the best were exquisitely made and very expensive. The Special Club Roadster cost £21 - 7 - 6 which was a lot of money to pay for a bicycle in 1884.

The 'Alert', 'Centaur', 'Cogent', 'Coventry Express', 'Will o' the Wisp' and most of the others have long since disappeared but names like Humber, Rover and Triumph are familiar to us today.

The high bicycle was such a fine machine that cycling became much more popular as a sport and pastime. Cycling clubs were started, and by 1880 there were as many as two hundred and thirty clubs up and down the country. Many were based in cities, which were smaller than they are today. It was very easy to ride out of London at weekends to the countryside through quiet villages which are now part of the city itself. Clubs with names like the 'Pickwick', the 'Happy-go-luckies' and the 'Cotswold Nondescripts' suggest that they all had a very good time.

Men in those days were careful in matters of dress and many clubs had their own uniform which members were expected to wear. The Cyclists' Touring Club, which was founded in 1878 and is now the oldest touring club in the world, appointed an official tailor. The uniform consisted of a dark green Devonshire serge jacket, knickerbockers and 'Stanley helmet with small peak'. Later, the colour was changed to grey because green showed up every speck of dirt. Cyclists liked to pose with their smart machines in photographers' studios or in informal groups outside country inns. Cycling was thirsty work, especially in summer when the roads were very dusty, so it is hardly surprising that so many photographs were taken outside inns which were then open all day.

A club run in the 1880s was a fine sight, rather like a troop of cavalry on wheels. The captain often carried a bugle which he blew to signal 'mount', 'dismount' or 'slacken speed'. The members riding a variety of Ordinaries and tricycles carried whistles, bells or pneumatic horns called *cyclornes* to warn people of their approach. This was necessary because in the days before the motor car, people almost always walked in the middle of the road, and on warm summer days dogs liked to sleep in peaceful village streets where today it is dangerous to cross the road.

Philip York II
Squire of Erddig, Circa 1885

Ninety years ago there were few travellers on country roads at night, and people preferred to stay close to home unless there was a good reason to be out. Old people could remember hearing stories when they were young about highwaymen and there was a feeling that it was best not to be out on dark nights. Roads that were quiet and peaceful during the day were quite deserted at night except perhaps for the village doctor in his gig or on horseback. There were no street lights in villages, no car headlights and very few signposts. It was very much like the blackout during the war when it was very easy to get lost or wander off the road into a ditch.

Cyclists out for the day often found themselves miles from home as darkness fell so it was essential to carry candle or oil lamps. A single lamp gave a rather dim light but a group of cyclists could see well enough and it was more agreeable to be with friends than alone on a dark, deserted road. Riding a high bicycle was difficult enough during the day and it must have been a hair-raising experience in the dark. Ruts and potholes were difficult to see and it was that much easier to 'come a cropper' or crash into one of the many toll gates which still existed.

In spite of the hazards, cycling at night must have been very enjoyable. The riders had the road to themselves and there was the warm, friendly smell in the air of paraffin lamps as they pedalled on through the quiet night.

A man walking with a companion along a Sussex road described the scene very well:
"Arriving at the village where we were to spend the night we encountered quite an array of cyclists speeding with flying wheels towards Brighton. One moment a blaze of lamps rounding the corner, the next, a blank darkness and the sound of ringing bells as they swept past us down the road."

The Ordinary bicycle suited daring young men, but there were many cyclists who preferred something safer. The design of tricycles was greatly improved and although they were very expensive and took up a lot of room when not in use, more and more cyclists rode them. For a time, the three-wheeler seemed to have a better future than the bicycle. Because of this, several new bicycles were designed which were safer than the Ordinary. The Xtraordinary was designed so that the rider was seated further back and the danger of being thrown over the handlebars was reduced. The 'Kangaroo' and 'Facile' were 'dwarf' ordinaries with very much smaller driving wheels pedalled through gears to make up for the reduced size. Because the riding position was much lower these machines were safer and were very successful. In 1884, G. Smith rode a hundred miles in under seven hours on a Kangaroo.

Although the railway had been opened as early as 1840, stage coaches ran daily between London and Brighton until 1890. It was a sport for rich men who loved driving horses and wanted to keep old traditions alive. In 1888, James Selby, who was the most famous 'whip' of them all, won a £1,000 wager by driving his coach 'Old Times' from the White Horse Cellars in Piccadilly to the Old Ship at Brighton, and back, in the record time of seven hours and fifty minutes. Thirteen teams of four horses were used and the quickest change was made in only 47 seconds! No other coach ever managed to beat this and many cyclists tried without success, until in 1890 F. W. Shorland on a 'Facile' fitted with the new pneumatic tyres finally beat the fifty-two horses with a time of seven hours and nineteen minutes. Many great cyclists have set later records on this famous road. A record was set in 1977 when P. Griffiths rode the 106 miles in four hours 13 minutes.

In the 1870s and 80s, cyclists were still a rare sight in remote country districts and created a great deal of interest, not all of which was very friendly. Practical jokes were rougher then than they are now and village lads with nothing much to do on their days off work sometimes amused themselves by ambushing cyclists in some quiet lane. Dogs were set at the riders or sticks poked through the wheels. Even worse, a thin wire might be stretched across the road between two trees causing a frightful crash.

There was ill feeling between cyclists and many drivers of horse-drawn vehicles who often deliberately ran cyclists off the road. We can be sure that some 'scorchers' were as much to blame as the horsemen. There were those who enjoyed bearing down on carriages and pedestrians at high speed and the situation became bad enough for the Bicycle Union to issue a Code of Conduct in 1878.

The police were particularly hostile to racing cyclists and massed-start road racing was eventually banned. Since then racing on the roads has been more or less limited to time-trials – riders setting out at minute intervals racing against the clock.

Although the 'dwarf' ordinaries were safer than the high bicycle a new machine was being developed which soon made the 'Penny-farthing' as obsolete as the boneshaker.

The new safety bicycles had wheels of nearly equal size and the rear wheel was driven by a chain. They were primitive versions of the modern bicycle. The first designs were in many ways inferior to the ordinary bicycle but progress was so rapid that the ordinary was soon abandoned. Safety bicycles were easier to ride and the gearing no longer depended on the length of the rider's legs but could be easily altered. At first, as engineers experimented with new ideas, many odd-looking machines were made. The 'Whippet' had a spring frame which made it more comfortable to ride on bumpy roads, and some machines were made with bamboo frames to save weight. The Rover Safety of 1885 looked much more like a modern machine and proved its superiority over all other types in a 100-mile race

in the same year. The modern 'diamond' frame was developed from the Rover and was to appear with the 1890 Humber.

In 1888, a veterinary surgeon called John Boyd Dunlop patented his pneumatic tyre. It was probably the most important invention in the history of cycling and of all modern road vehicles. Compared with solid tyres, riding on air was a miracle of speed, comfort and lightness, and although punctures happened even more often then than they do now, the new tyres were an immediate success. Today, millions of cars and lorries use pneumatic tyres and many people are surprised to learn that they were first used on bicycles.

Many important inventions are due to the cycle industry. In 1903 the first successful aeroplane was designed by two bicycle makers called Wilbur and Orville Wright.

The 'diamond' frame, first made by the Humber Company in 1890 was a big improvement on other designs and most other makers quickly copied it. As a result, bicycles began to look very much the same although they varied considerably in details and quality. The diamond frame was the end result of years of experience and was such a brilliant invention that it has remained basically the same to this day and it is doubtful whether it will ever be improved upon.

The top tube or crossbar was unsuitable for lady riders and was replaced by a down tube which on most early models was curved or 'looped'. Ladies' bicycles are good enough for everyday use but the absence of a crossbar makes them less strong and rigid. This is why women racing cyclists always ride men's bicycles.

A famous exception to the diamond frame was the Dursley-Pedersen which was designed on completely different principles by a Danish engineer called Mikael Pedersen who lived at Dursley in Gloucestershire. Instead of a normal leather saddle these machines were fitted with hammock-type saddles and were real lightweights. Harry Green, a famous cyclist at the turn of the century, used a Dursley-Pedersen on several record-breaking rides. Pedersen, who in many ways was ahead of his time, designed a collapsible bicycle for the army which weighed only 17lb. Naturally the army saw no use for such a machine at the time, although in both world wars bicycles were used, including a folding machine by paratroopers.

During the 1890s many improvements made the bicycle more comfortable and easier to ride. Freewheels enabled riders to coast down hills without pedalling, and brakes which had been primitive in the early days, became really efficient. Pneumatic tyres made cycling comfortable for the first time. For a brief period, cycling became fashionable among the upper classes. Ladies and gentlemen liked to ride around the parks and on a fine day as many as three thousand elegant riders could be seen in Hyde Park alone. Although it is doubtful whether many of them ever strayed very far from the parks, they made cycling respectable for the first time. Soon, almost everyone who could afford to buy a bicycle took up the new craze. Unfortunately, like most fashions, 'cyclomania' did not last long. By 1900 the upper classes grew tired of their bicycles which were left to rust in their coachhouses. Motoring was soon to become the new craze and the bicycle has been ignored by smart people ever since.

Some of the finest bicycles were made during this period when England was the workshop of the world. The Humber, Lea Francis and Marston Sunbeam were made by craftsmen to a standard of workmanship almost unknown today. In an age of mass production when so many things we use lack interest and are not made to last, it is worth looking at these beautiful machines. They were made in an age when people took great pride in their work and gained a great deal of pleasure and satisfaction from their skill.

Club uniforms went out of fashion with the penny-farthing. In the old days the bicycle had been a man's machine, but during the 1890s the safety bicycle made it possible for women to take to the wheel. As cycling became popular with both men and women, more informal wear was preferred. Men wore normal country clothes – comfortable Norfolk jackets and breeches – but women found their everyday clothes to be quite unsuitable. Ankle-length skirts, five yards around the hem, looked very feminine but made pedalling difficult and tight corsets restricted breathing.

The well-dressed lady cyclist wore loose-fitting merino wool underwear and silk knickerbockers, a skirt three inches from the ground and two and a half yards round the hem which was weighted to keep it in place. An Eton jacket or short coat completed the costume. Hats were always worn – felt in winter and a straw boater in summer.

Some women thought this dress too restricting and wore 'bloomers' instead of a skirt. This was called 'rational' dress and although these very baggy bloomers reached well below the knee many people thought them to be indecent. Women wearing 'rationals' were often barred from hotel dining rooms and even had stones thrown at them by other women.

Eventually, rational dress was accepted and the movement towards the emancipation of women was certainly helped by the first lady cyclists. We tend to think of Victorian and Edwardian women as rather helpless creatures but this is obviously untrue as many of them were quite capable of repairing and looking after their bicycles. "Any woman who can use a needle and scissors can use other tools as well", wrote a lady cyclist in 1896. Only a few years later, women in factories were making the guns and ammunition for the British Army in the Great War.

During the early years of this century, life in towns and villages was carried on at the same leisurely pace that had existed for centuries. Most places were in reach of a railway station so that heavy goods as well as passengers travelled by train leaving the roads almost free of traffic. A ten-mile radius from home was as far as a horse-drawn vehicle could be expected to go in a day so nearly all road traffic was local.

The bicycle suited this way of life perfectly and it is no wonder that it was so popular. Variable-speed gears became available and although the best machines were expensive a good bicycle could be bought for as little as £5. Ordinary people enjoyed mobility for the first time and all kinds of people discovered the advantages of the bicycle. It was safe, very much cheaper to keep than a horse, and it was faster. It is difficult to believe that only 70 odd years ago the bicycle was the fastest vehicle on the roads.

Cycle touring became very popular and many people were able to explore the countryside for the first time.

Tramps were more numerous in those days and ladies who were worried about being pestered or robbed were advised to take a pair of spotted carriage dogs or greyhounds with them, which seems an attractive idea. At the end of the day, ostlers at country hotels could be relied on to clean and oil one's bicycle and there was little need to carry much luggage – it would have arrived by railway from the previous day's stopping point.

At night, cyclists still used oil lamps but the new acetylene lamps which gave a much brighter light were gaining ground, although they could be troublesome. These superb lamps, which worked by dripping water on calcium carbide to produce acetylene gas were also used on the first motor cars.

When 'horseless carriages' first appeared on the roads in the 1890s they were not taken very seriously. They were unreliable and were given a speed limit of four miles per hour because they were thought to frighten the horses. The police were even more hostile to motorists than they had been to the early cyclists and most people thought cars were a joke.

The speed limit was lifted in 1900 and the prospect of swift, comfortable travelling began to be realised. Motoring became fashionable with wealthy people who, a few years earlier, had been keen cyclists and bicycles were left rusting in sheds as the new fashion spread. As cars and motor cycles rapidly increased in number cycling became less popular – the bicycle became the 'push bike', a poor man's vehicle, only to be used by people unable to buy a car or motor cycle. In the 1950s and 60s as the living standard of ordinary people improved, millions more cars poured onto the roads and lorries were increasingly used to carry heavy goods. Most of the branch railway lines were closed because they were losing money and people in country districts became dependent on motor transport.

As a result, roads that not long ago were peaceful and safe are noisy and dangerous and our towns and cities are congested with traffic. Although some people think that the growth in motor transport will continue indefinitely, there are signs that this will not happen. Fuel costs are rising and in large cities many people are realising that it is cheaper, quicker and healthier to ride a bicycle, or even to walk.

After years of neglect, the humble bicycle seems likely to become popular again. Apart from the congestion caused by motor vehicles, people are beginning to realise that exercise is essential if they are to keep fit and healthy. Businessmen on small-wheeled folding bicycles can be seen pedalling rather slowly and laboriously through Hyde Park where long ago the dandies rode their hobby horses. Today's Park riders on their funny bicycles may not be as elegant as the fashionable riders on their beautiful machines of eighty years ago but they benefit from the exercise and often arrive at their offices without the strain and frustration that motorists increasingly have to put up with.

Many people are afraid of cycling in towns because of the heavy traffic but is is nearly always possible to avoid crowded roads and find a quiet route through side streets. Many towns are beginning to provide separate cycle tracks and British Rail allow bicycles to be carried free on most trains. In years to come, cycling is almost certain to be a popular form of personal transport once again. But it would be a pity to think of the bicycle only as a cheap and convenient way of getting to and from work. In spite of crowded noisy roads, cycling is still an enjoyable and healthy pastime for people of all ages.

At a time when many people only want to go faster and faster, the bicycle is still the best way to enjoy the countryside at a speed in scale with our small island. There may soon be a new golden age of cycling and the bicycle could even become King of the Road again. But before cycling can become really popular, we all need to learn that there is more to travelling than sheer speed and that a more gentle pace of life is good for our minds and bodies. We would soon discover the rewards of using our own muscle power rather than relying on machines to do everything for us.

Useful Addresses

Cyclists' Touring Club

Cotterell House
Meadrow
Godalming
Surrey

Southern Veteran-Cycle Club

8 Shrubbery Road
Gravesend
Kent

Youth Hostel Association

29 John Adam Street
London
WC2

Collections of Cycles

The National Trust

Snowshill Manor
Nr. Broadway
Worcestershire

The National Trust

Erddig House
Wrexham
Clwyd
N. Wales

The Science Museum

South Kensington
London

The Pinkerton Bicycle Museum

Arbury Hall
Nuneaton
Warwickshire

Printed in Great Britain by Tabro Litho, St Ives, Cambs
Reproduced by C L Enterprises, Fenstanton, Cambs
Bound by Suffolk Print Finishers, Bury St Edmunds

65p (U.K. only)

POLITICAL SCIENCE | **Public Policy** | Energy Policy

Climate change will force us to distribute energy and regulate the system. But who will control the system? This unique moment in history provides an unprecedented opening for a deeper transformation of the energy system, and thus, an opportunity to transform society. *Revolutionary Power* shows us how.

"Who knew that a book on energy justice would be so captivating? *Revolutionary Power* is a deeply personal, spirit-filled, and accessible read into the struggles and practical policy solutions to return our toxic energy systems to the commons and address a legacy of environmental racism. It is an inspiring guide that makes energy and energy justice easy to understand and radical ideas doable."

—**Denise Fairchild**, President/Chief Executive Officer, Emerald Cities Collaborative; coeditor of *Energy Democracy*

"The story of environmental racism and climate change begins with the plunder, pillaging, and extraction of our land and labor. It is personal for those of us of African and Indigenous ancestry. *Revolutionary Power* takes us on a journey of love and gives history, context, and life to the frontline struggle for reclamation and community ownership of renewable energy and the future of our communities. Shalanda Baker's story is our story and makes clear that the descendants of extraction must be the 'architects and beneficiaries of the new energy system.' This important literary contribution honors our ancestors while lifting the complexity, sophistication, and frontline-centered solutions of the climate justice movement."

—**Elizabeth C. Yeampierre**, Executive Director, UPROSE

Cover design by Maryn Schmoll
Cover art courtesy of iStockphoto.com

ISLANDPRESS
Washington | Covelo
www.islandpress.org

All Island Press books are printed on environmentally responsible materials.

BRENTWOOD

ISBN/85122/156/4